I Introduction
Technology

I.1 What is technology?

I.2 Archimedes: a great inventor

I.3 How science shapes technology

I.4 How technology shapes science

I.5 Discussion questions

I.1 What is technology?

Think for a moment about what it might be like to live in the 14th century. Imagine that you can travel back in time and that you find yourself in a small European village in 1392.

What do you think you would find? How would you cook your food? Would you use an oven, a fire, or a microwave? How would you eat your food? Do you think you could use a plastic cup to drink your milk? How would you go from one city to the next? Could you get on a train, or would you have to walk, or would you ride a horse? How could you send a message to your mom to tell her that you'll be late for dinner? Could you e-mail her, or could you call her on your cell phone?

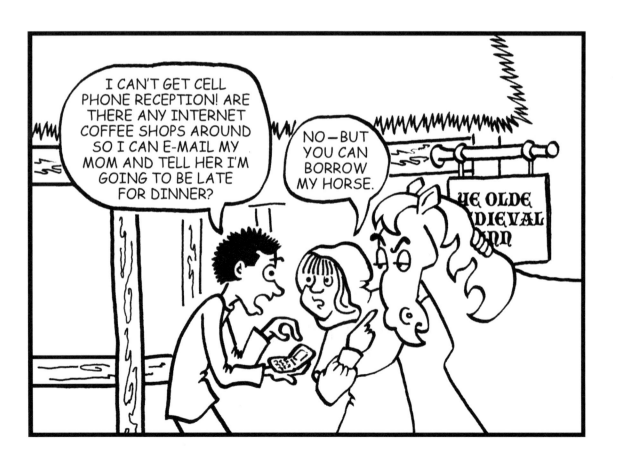

How would you get clothes? Could you shop at a 14th century mall or on the internet? And what would your clothes be made of? Do you think you could find pink spandex shorts, or would they have to be made of brown cotton? Think for a moment about how different everything would be if you were to live in the 14th century.

Many of the items that you use today are a result of **technology**. Your cell phone, microwave oven, washing machine, and plastic cup are all the result of a combination of scientific discoveries and engineering. This combination of scientific discoveries and engineering has allowed people to invent products that have improved the way people live. Technological advances have improved our health, the food we eat, the clothes we wear, how we travel, and how we communicate with one another. There are a few drawbacks to some aspects of technology (such as pollution), but overall, technology has greatly improved many aspects of living for most people.

The word "technology" comes from the Greek words *techne*, which means "craft," and *logy*, which means "scientific study of." So *technology* means the "scientific study of craft." Craft, in this case, means any method or invention that allows humans to control or adapt to their environment.

I.2 Archimedes: a great inventor

How did technology get started? Inventions and tool making have been around for as long as human beings have walked the earth. But modern technology began once scientific thought (philosophy), astronomy, and mathematics began to blend together; this occurred sometime after the 15th century.

The first inventor who combined engineering with science was **Archimedes of Syracuse** (287 B.C.-212 B.C.). He is credited with inventing the **Archimedean screw,** which is used for raising water. The Archimedean screw is still used in Egypt today. He is also credited with inventing the **cross-staff,** which is used in astronomy. And he invented the **odometer,** which measures how far someone has traveled.

The most famous story about Archimedes is the one in which he was told by the king to find out whether the king's crown was made of solid gold. He had to figure out a way to test the crown in order to see whether it was made of gold, and he had to do so without melting it. This was a puzzle for Archimedes. It is said that one day he noticed that his body would displace the bath water. Seeing this, he realized that he could use the displacement of water as a way to measure the crown's volume (and thus its density upon weighing it). As the story

goes, it was at this point that Archimedes jumped out of the tub and ran through the streets naked; as he ran, he shouted, "Eureka! I have found it!" No one is certain whether the story is true, but it does give you an idea of how exciting new discoveries in technology can be!

I.3 How science shapes technology

Before formal scientific disciplines (such as chemistry, physics, astronomy, and biology) were defined, many early inventors simply experimented with items around them and tried to come up with ways to improve their lives. Inventions and discoveries often happened by accident. Glass, for example, is said to have been discovered by Phoenician sailors in 4000 B.C. According to the ancient story, the sailors were cooking on nitrate blocks. The blocks were melted by the fire, and they mixed with the sand below. This created a crude glass. No one could have guessed at the time, but these sailors helped pave the way for Galileo and others to use telescopes for observing the stars.

The earliest star gazers had no way to see beyond what they could observe in the sky with their own eyes. For these early astronomers, the technology for seeing beyond our solar system and galaxy did not yet exist. In the early 1600s, Galileo Galilei observed the heavens through the first telescope. It took both the scientific idea that glass could magnify far away objects and the craft of glass making in order for the first telescope to be invented. Improvements in how much a telescope could magnify were accelerated by Sir Isaac Newton's ideas regarding using a curved mirror rather than glass for the lens. Because Newton understood the science of light, called **optics**, he was able to add to the technological advance of the telescope. Science shapes technology, and without an understanding of basic scientific principles and without the gathering of new scientific facts, technological advances in any area would be impossible.

I.4 How technology shapes science

Looking at it from the other end, how does technology shape science? Going back to Galileo and Newton, how do you think the telescope has changed our understanding of not only our own solar system, but of the whole universe?

The telescope ushered in a new and fascinating scientific discipline that we now call **astronomy**. Astronomy is the scientific study of the planets, stars, and other objects in the universe. Before the telescope, no one had ever observed a nebula, for example, and no one knew how many planets were in our solar system. Without the technology of the telescope, much of what we have discovered about the universe would still be unknown.

The telescope also opened up many ideas and changed the way people thought about **cosmology**. Cosmology is the study of the universe. It would be very difficult to study the universe if we had no way to look beyond our own planet. The technology of the telescope brought modern cosmology into the arena of serious scientific study. The telescope enabled scientists to measure, predict, and quantify many features of the universe. By applying mathematics to careful observations generated by the use of telescopes, scientists changed the way people thought about the universe and themselves.

I.5 Discussion questions

1. Think about a piece of technology that you use today, such as a cell phone or a television. List all of the materials that the item is composed of. For example, does the item contain plastic, metal (what kind?), glass, etc.?

___
___
___
___
___
___
___
___
___
___

2. Now think about one of those materials, and try to answer the following questions. Use library or internet resources to research the answers.

    a) How is it made?

_____

_____

_____

_____

    b) Where is it made?

_____

_____

_____

_____

    c) Who designed it?

_____

_____

_____

_____

3. Think about the process for designing and making the material.

   a) Which scientific disciplines are involved in this process?

   _____

   _____

   _____

   _____

   _____

   _____

   b) Explain how chemistry or physics helped in creating the piece of technology you described.

   _____

   _____

   _____

   _____

   _____

   _____

   _____

   _____

1 Small-Scale Science Technology

1.1 "Seeing" atoms

1.2 Scanning tunneling microscope

1.3 Atomic force microscope

1.4 Nanotechnology

1.5 Activity

1.1 "Seeing" atoms

How small are atoms? Atoms are too small to even picture! The cells that make up living things are small, but even the smallest living cell is made up of billions of atoms! If atoms are so small, how can we be sure they exist?

For a long time, the answer to that question was, Well, we have lots of experimental evidence that makes it seem like atoms exist, but we can't really see atoms because they are just too small! However, in the 1980s a new microscope technology was invented. This new device was called a **scanning tunneling microscope,** or STM. An STM makes it possible to "see" atoms.

1.2 Scanning tunneling microscope

A scanning tunneling microscope is not a typical microscope. It does not work with light or lenses, and you don't look through it. In fact, when using an STM, you do not actually "see" the atoms, at least, not in the way that you are looking at this page in front of you.

An STM works by "scanning" the surface of an object and then projecting an image of the surface on a computer monitor or other screen. The STM has a metal probe called a **stylus** that actually does the scanning. The stylus is extremely sharp; it comes to a point that is only one atom wide! This stylus moves very close to the surface of the object being scanned. The gap between the tip of the stylus and the object is about as wide as one atom, or it may be even smaller.

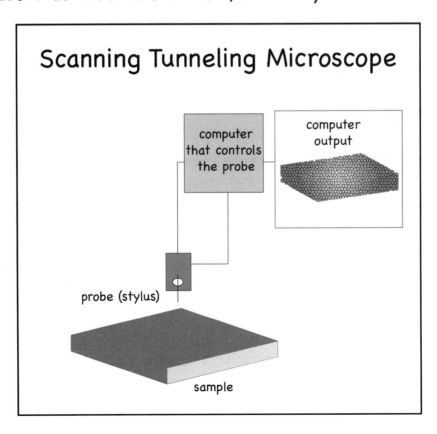

The STM works by passing the stylus back and forth over the surface of the object that is being scanned. The moving stylus is controlled by a computer. Human beings are not precise enough to keep the stylus at the right distance from the scanning surface. As the stylus moves, it "picks up" electrons from the surface of the object. The electrons show where the atoms in the object are located. The signals created by these electrons are strengthened and then projected onto a monitor to create an image.

An STM can produce phenomenal images of a surface, but it has another amazing function. An STM can be used to "grab" individual atoms! The computer controlling the STM can then move the atoms to specific locations. In 1990, researchers at IBM used an STM to grab individual xenon atoms. It took over 20 hours, but they were able to arrange 35 atoms into the letters I, B, and M to make the smallest company logo ever.

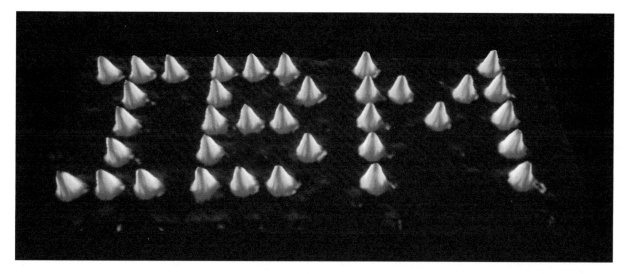

Xenon atoms written on a surface spelling "IBM"
(reprinted with permission from IBM Corporate Archives)

Since then, researchers have been working on ways to move atoms around more quickly. They are discovering ways to make incredibly tiny structures, one atom at a time.

1.3 Atomic force microscope

One of the drawbacks of the early scanning tunneling microscopes was that they could only be used to scan objects that conduct electricity easily, like metals. Therefore, they could not be used to create images of substances that were not conductors of electricity, such as plastics or living tissues. In the years since STMs were invented, several other types of probe microscopes have been developed. They work in slightly different ways, but the basic principle remains similar; the microscopes allow scientists to get an extremely close-up image of an object. One type is called an Atomic Force Microscope, or AFM. An AFM can scan many different types of surfaces, including metals and nonmetals.
Like an STM, an AFM has a very short tip. But instead of picking up electrons like an STM, an AFM can "see" atoms by just bumping into them (that is, by measuring the **force** between an atom and the tip). Because everything is made of atoms, an AFM can see all kinds of things, not just conductors.

1.4 Nanotechnology

The science of designing and working with extremely small things is called **nanotechnology**. The *nano* in nanotechnology means "**nanometer**," and so *nanotechnology* means "building things that are nanometers in size." A nanometer is one billionth of a meter; that is, it takes one billion nanometers to equal one meter. Remember that scientists use the metric system to measure things. A meter is the standard metric unit for length. One thousandth of a meter is called a millimeter. One millimeter is about as wide as the line you would draw with a sharp pencil. A nanometer is a **much** smaller unit. One millimeter is equal to one million nanometers! An atom is less than a nanometer across, so a device like an STM or an AFM is an essential tool for scientists who want to visualize and pick up individual atoms.

Some nanotechnology researchers are developing new ways of using various types of STMs and AFMs. Biologists can use a special type of AFM to look at proteins and other compounds one molecule at a time. Computer makers can produce super-miniature computer circuits. Medical researchers can examine how a particular medicine affects specific cells. Chemists and materials scientists are using nanotechnology techniques to develop completely new substances that have never before been made.

One of the problems with nanotechnology is that it is difficult to use "big" machines to make such incredibly tiny structures. So some engineers are working on designing "nanomachines." These extremely tiny machines might someday be able to build very, very tiny robots called "nanobots."

One nanobot would be too small to get a job done quickly all by itself. However, if millions of nanobots could work together, they might be able to do amazing things. Researchers think that teams of nanobots might be able to do microscopic surgery inside a patient's body. Some groups of nanobots might be programmed to build objects by arranging atoms so precisely that there would be no waste. Other nanobots might even be designed to build more nanobots to replace those that wear out!

Compared to other areas of science, like chemistry and biology, nanotechnology is a very new area of research. Working with such small things is still very slow and difficult work. However, as the science of nanotechnology continues to develop, researchers will certainly find faster and easier ways to manipulate very small structures, including individual atoms.

1.5 Activity

1. You will need the following materials:
    - A firm object, such as your text book
    - A soft object, such as a small pillow or cotton ball
    - A pen
    - A piece of paper
    - A blindfold

This exercise will give you some idea as to how an STM operates.

❶ Place the hard object on a table (or other flat surface) where you are comfortable writing.

❷ Set the paper on the table next to the object. If you are right-handed, you will want the paper to the right of the object. If you are left-handed, you will want the paper to the left of the object.

❸ Take the pen, and place it near the paper where you can easily find it and pick it up.

❹ Take the blindfold, and place it over your eyes.

❺ With your non-writing hand, feel the surface of the table until you touch the book or firm object.

❻ Now take your index finger, and point it downward toward the object on the table. Your index finger is your "stylus."

❼ Move your finger (horizontally) over the object in a straight line, and at the same time, record with your writing hand what your feeling hand is touching. Draw just the first line of the object your finger is touching.

❽ Next, move your finger slightly downward, and going in the opposite direction, scan your second line.

❾ Repeat your scans until you reach the bottom of the object.

❿ Repeat steps one through nine with the soft object and a new piece of paper.

Scan the object back and forth with your finger.

Using a pen, record on the paper what your "scanning finger" is feeling.

Questions

1. How well do your drawings represent the real objects?

___

___

___

___

2. What are some of the problems you found when trying to "image" the objects in this way?

___

___

___

___

3. Based on your observations that you made with your "human STM," list some of the problems that you think an actual STM might encounter.

4. Based on your observations that you made with your "human STM," think about some ways that you might solve some of the problems you encountered.

Seeing Atoms With X-rays
Technology

2.1 Introduction

2.2 Crystal structure

2.3 X-ray crystallography

2.4 Doing X-ray crystallography

2.5 Making models from X-ray data

2.6 Activities

2.1 Introduction

Do you remember the formula for water? It's H_2O, which means each molecule of water is a chemical combination of two hydrogen atoms and one oxygen atom. We usually picture water molecules looking something like this:

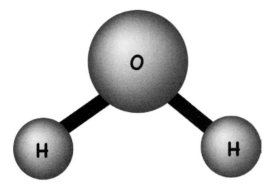

Why do we use this particular shape? Why don't we arrange the atoms in a straight line, like this?

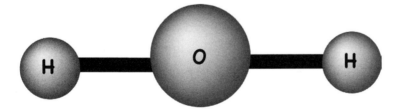

Why don't we picture the water molecule as being folded up, like this?

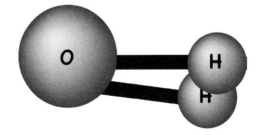

How can scientists be sure which shape is the right one for H_2O?

Remember that atoms—and even molecules—are far too small to see with your eyes. Because chemists can't actually see molecules, they have developed other ways of determining the shapes of different molecules. One of the most common methods is called **X-ray crystallography**. X-ray crystallography lets chemists picture what molecules look like.

2.2 Crystal structure

Have you ever looked at salt up close? We usually think of salt as being a sort of grainy, white powder. However, if you look at individual grains of salt with a microscope, they actually look like very tiny cubes! These cubes are tiny crystals.

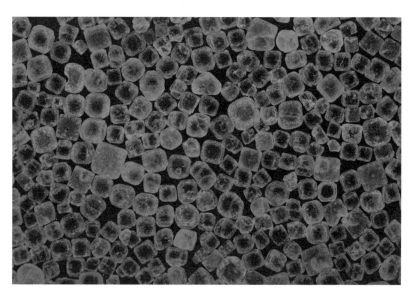
© Igor Marx | Dreamstime.com

Small as these crystals are, they are still made up of many, many atoms.

Solid substances are commonly made up of crystals. Most rocks, minerals, and metals are crystals. Crystals have a very orderly atomic structure. The overall shape of a crystal has a lot to do with the way bonds form between the atoms that make up a crystal.

For instance, salt is made up of sodium ions and chlorine ions that are attracted to each other. A grain of salt is simply an organized collection of sodium and chlorine ions. One grain of salt may be made up of millions of sodium and chlorine atoms, but they are sorted out into this very orderly structure. The overall structure of the grain of salt is determined by the bonds that form between the atoms.

Diamonds are another example of a crystal structure. Diamonds are made up of carbon atoms. They form a pyramid-like shape, and each carbon atom is connected to four other carbon atoms. Again, the overall crystal shape is determined by the bonds that form between the atoms that make up the crystal.

Many other substances can also be formed into crystals. Ice is crystallized water. Sugar can be crystallized into rock candy. These are fairly simple molecules, but more complex molecules

Diamond crystal. David Keller

can also be formed into crystals. For example, protein molecules are made up of hundreds (or even thousands!) of atoms, but they too, can be formed into crystals. This allows crystallographers to study the shape of these larger molecules by using a technique called X-ray crystallography.

2.3 X-ray crystallography

What is X-ray crystallography? *Crystallography* literally means "crystal drawing" ("graph" comes from the Greek word *graphein*, which means "to write" or "to draw"]. So *X-ray crystallography* means "to draw crystals with X-rays."

An X-ray is a very short wavelength of light. X-rays travel in waves in the same way that visible light does. Because X-rays are essentially the same thing as visible light, they can be reflected, scattered, and bent, just like visible light.

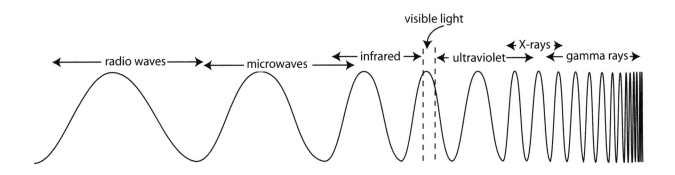

How does X-ray crystallography work? If you shine a flashlight into a mirror, the light will get reflected, or "scattered," by the mirror. You can see where the light bounces off the mirror if you look behind you. But what if you didn't know that the mirror was there and you could look only behind you? Well, by looking at how the light scatters, you can "detect" the presence of the mirror and you can determine where the mirror is located.

The same thing will happen if you pass X-rays through a crystal. The X-rays will be scattered by the atoms in the crystal, and scientists can detect this scattering. By analyzing the scattering of the X-rays, scientists can make a map of where the atoms in the crystal are located.

Why can't crystallographers just use visible light to visualize molecules? Crystallographers can't use wavelengths of visible light because the wavelengths of visible light are actually longer than the width of the atoms that they are trying to view! Because X-rays have a shorter wavelength than visible light, scientists can pass X-rays through crystals. In this way, X-rays can be used to view the structure of the atomic bonds inside crystals.

2.4 Doing X-ray crystallography

The first step in X-ray crystallography is developing a high quality crystal. For some substances, such as salt, this isn't so difficult. For complex molecules, like proteins, it is much harder, because proteins are made up of many atoms. A crystallographer will often spend days, or even weeks, making sure that he or she has a crystal without any flaws. An imperfect crystal won't give a crystallographer an accurate picture of the structure of the molecular bonds. Once a researcher is satisfied with the quality of the crystal, he or she can begin the process of X-ray crystallography.

A crystallographer's next step is to shoot X-rays at the crystal. The X-rays reflect off the atoms in the crystal similar to the way light rays are scattered off of a mirror. The X-rays that are bounced off the atoms are picked up by a special X-ray detector. This detector is connected to a computer that keeps track of the way the X-rays are scattered. These scattered reflections give information about where the atoms in the crystal are located with respect to one another. The structure for DNA was revealed by X-ray crystallography.

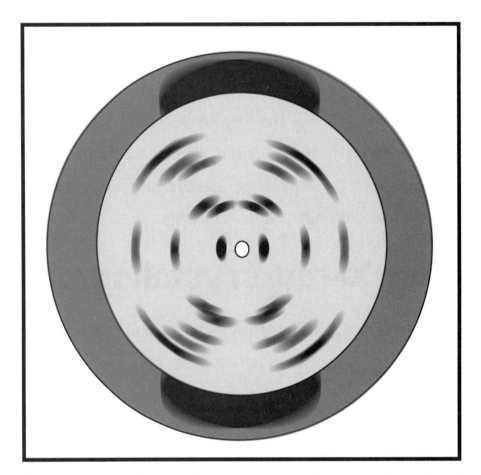

Representation of an X-ray picture for DNA

2.5 Making models from X-ray data

A computer is used to create a model of what the bonds between the atoms making up the molecule look like. This process takes time to complete. A crystallographer often needs to complete several trials in order to be sure that his or her model is accurate. The result is a computer model of the shape of the molecule.

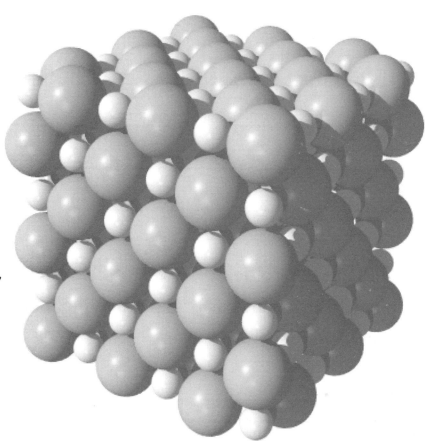

Why do crystallographers have to use crystals to make a model of a molecule? Why can't they just use a single molecule? Well, even though X-rays have a short enough wavelength to "view" a single molecule, it would take too long! Remember that crystals have the same structure repeated throughout. Using a crystal gives a larger "target" to aim at. Because the molecules making up the crystal all have exactly the same shape, the X-rays are reflected off the crystal in exactly the same way. Even if the X-rays bounce off of a slightly different part of the crystal, the picture formed by the computer will look the same. Using X-rays can allow scientists to make accurate models of molecules. An accurate model of a molecule gives scientists information about how different substances will behave, and it also gives them information about the types of bonds that the molecules can form.

2.6 Activities

1. Think of ways that you can "see" the shapes of things by using light, without actually looking at the objects directly. Write your ideas below.

   _____
   _____
   _____
   _____

2. Place several objects close to a blank wall or next to a piece of paper. Shine a flashlight on the objects, and observe the shadows. Draw the shadows you see.

3. Place three dots (1 inch or larger) on a mirror. With your back to the mirror, shine a flashlight toward the mirror, and see if you can "detect" the dots. Have a friend rearrange the dots, and see if you can tell how they have been rearranged.

3 Hard Water Technology

3.1 What is "hard water"?

3.2 The problem of hard water

3.3 Softening water

3.4 Discussion questions

3.1 What is "hard water"?

Water is a liquid, right? So how can it be "hard"? Ice is water in solid form. But ice is not what people usually mean when they say water is "hard."

Water is very useful for dissolving certain substances. When you put table salt crystals in water, it looks like the salt disappears. But the salt doesn't really disappear; only the crystals disappear. The salt crystals are **dissolved**, or broken up, by the water. Table salt is made of sodium ions and chlorine ions. When table salt is put into water, the water breaks apart the ions, and the salt crystals disappear. But the water is still full of sodium ions and chlorine ions!

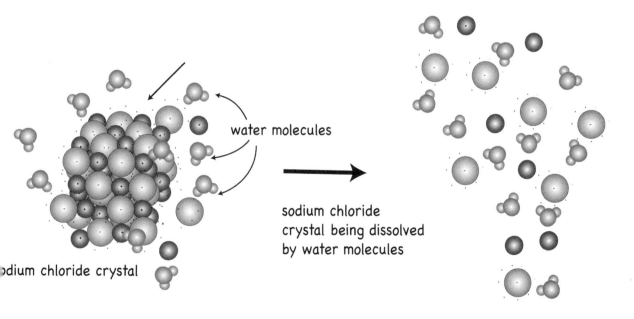

Water easily dissolves things like table salt and sugar. But other kinds of things, like minerals, can also be dissolved in water. Water in lakes, rivers, and wells can contain minerals like calcium and magnesium. Even water that comes out of your kitchen tap is probably not "pure water." It has small amounts of different minerals dissolved in it, and these dissolved minerals are the cause of "hard" water.

3.2 The problem of hard water

Most parts of the United States have hard water. The minerals dissolved in the water usually come from rocks. The water in rivers, lakes, wells, and reservoirs come in contact with rocks that contain minerals, and because water is such a great dissolver, the minerals dissolve right into the water supply. The most common minerals to be dissolved into water are calcium and magnesium. In some places, iron, aluminum, and other minerals are also common.

Why is hard water a problem? Minerals in water usually aren't harmful to people, plants, or animals. However, some people find that the minerals dissolved in hard water make the water taste bad.

Another problem is that hard water tends to leave its minerals behind. These left-behind minerals can build up and form a crusty, white deposit called **lime scale**. Lime scale can be annoying in your bathtub or shower. However, it can also cause a more serious problem; it can build up in pipes and clog them.

Also, soap does not lather up very well in hard water. The minerals in the hard water actually impede the soap's ability to work well. So it takes more soap or shampoo to feel clean when washing your body or hair. Dishes do not get as clean, especially in a dishwasher, and clothes do not get as clean in a washing machine. Also, the soap might be left behind (along with the minerals), coating the things being washed. This is what causes soap scum, or a bathtub ring.

3.3 Softening water

The good news is that hard water can be "softened." Water softeners are machines that remove the dissolved minerals from hard water. They do this through a fairly simple chemical reaction. Calcium and magnesium are very common ions to be dissolved in hard water. A water softener works by replacing these dissolved ions with different ions.

Water softeners have a canister where the water softening actually takes place. Inside this canister are thousands of tiny plastic beads. These beads contain sodium ions that allow the hard water to be softened. The hard water is pumped into the canister where a **displacement reaction** takes place. As the water flows past the plastic beads, calcium ions and magnesium ions are pulled out of the water, and they pass into the beads. As this happens, sodium ions are bumped out of the beads. This process might not remove all of the calcium and magnesium, but it certainly helps. The water leaving the canister is softer than the water coming in.

The plastic beads in the water softener canister need to be "recharged" from time to time. Another displacement reaction is responsible for this recharge.

Attached to the water softener canister is a tank called a **brine tank**. People using water softeners have to add salt to the brine tank regularly. The salt (NaCl) dissolves in the water in the brine tank. This very salty water is then pumped through the canister. As the salt water passes by the beads, the displacement reaction takes place. Sodium ions come out of the water and move into the beads. As the sodium ions move in, they kick out the calcium ions and magnesium ions. The calcium and magnesium ions that had originally made the water hard are then flushed out with the leftover salty water, and they go down the drain.

Hard water can be annoying, but it isn't life threatening. If you live in a regions that has naturally soft water, be thankful! If your family needs to use a water softener to help deal with hard water, you can be thankful for the engineers who applied chemistry to solve this common problem!

3.4 Discussion questions

1. How do you think the technology of water softeners has helped people live today?

___

2. What needed to be understood in chemistry before water softeners could be developed? (What minerals are dissolved in water? etc.)

___

3. Do you think soft water really makes soap lather more? Can you think of a way to "test" this idea, even if you don't have a water softener. (Hint - you might compare using purified water instead of tap water to wash your hands.)

4 Chemical Etching Technology

4.1 Acids and etching

4.2 Acids and art

4.3 The etching process

4.4 Other examples of etching

4.5 Discussion questions

4.1 Acids and etching

When you hear the word "acid," what comes to mind? Do you picture an incredibly strong chemical that will dissolve plastic and metal or that will melt a whole car? Science fiction stories give us this sort of picture of what acids are like, but not all acids are that strong. After all, even lemon juice is an acid, and you use it to make lemonade.

Acids are useful for **chemical etching**. Etching is a process of dissolving certain parts of a substance, without damaging other parts. An **etching agent** is a chemical that is used to etch a particular substance.

4.2 Acids and art

Hydrofluoric acid is an extremely strong acid that reacts with glass. It can't even be stored in a glass bottle because the bottle would be dissolved! Because it can react with glass, hydrofluoric acid can be used as an etching agent on glass.

© Robert Adrian Hillman | Dreamstime.com

Some artists create their works of art by using hydrofluoric acid to etch glass. To create a pattern, the artist covers up the parts of the glass that he or she doesn't want to damage. Then the artist brushes or wipes the acid over the surface of the glass. The acid does not affect the parts of the glass that are covered. The acid reacts with the uncovered glass and starts to dissolve it. In this way, the artist's pattern is etched into the glass. The extra hydrofluoric acid must then be rinsed off to stop the etching process. The result is a beautiful piece of artwork!

4.3 The etching process

The glass artwork etching described in the previous section explains the basic process of chemical etching. There are four basic steps to chemical etching:

- ❶ surface preparation
- ❷ masking
- ❸ etching
- ❹ rinsing

❶ **Surface preparation:** The surface that is to be etched (such as glass) should be cleaned of any oil or particles. It can be washed with soap and water, and it should be thoroughly dried.

❷ **Masking**: Masking is the process of covering the parts of the surface that should remain after the etching process. It is important that the mask does <u>not</u> react with the etching agent! Otherwise, it will not protect the surface during the etching process.

❸ **Etching**: The next step is the actual etching. An etching agent is applied to the masked surface. The etching agent is left in place for a period of time that is sufficient to allow it to react with the unmasked part of the surface.

❹ **Rinsing**: Finally, the surface must be rinsed. The etching agent must be removed from the masked surface to stop the etching process. Depending upon the etching agent used and the type of surface being etched, different rinsing chemicals might be needed. After the rinsing process is complete, the mask can be removed. The parts that were masked will be unaffected. The surface that was left uncovered will have dissolved away in the desired pattern.

4.4 Other examples of etching

There are several important applications of the etching process. We've already discussed the use of glass etching in artwork, but there are other materials, like metal, that can also be etched. Copper is an important metal that can be etched. While copper can be etched to create works of art, there is another useful application of etching copper: printed circuit boards (PCBs).

PCBs are common in many electronic devices, including computers. They are made up of layers of silicon that are pressed together to form a "wafer." A thin layer of copper is then pressed on top. Copper is an excellent conductor of electricity. Thus it is a useful metal for circuit boards and other electronic devices. This copper-coated silicon wafer is the substrate to be etched.

Engineers designing new circuits use computer programs to design the masks for PCBs. The mask is usually printed right onto the circuit board. (This is why they are called "printed" circuit boards!) The mask covers narrow lines of copper. Remember, only the parts that are masked will remain unaffected after the etching process.

The etching agent is applied to the masked surface. In factories where PCBs are mass-produced, the etching agent might be sprayed onto the surface or the surface might be dipped into the acid. The etching agent reacts with the copper layer, and it dissolves the unmasked metal.

Finally, the surface must be rinsed to remove the etching agent. Rinsing the acid off stops its reaction with the metal. Water is often used for rinsing because it can thin out the acid and wash it away. Once the etching agent has been thoroughly rinsed, the mask must then be washed off as well. Chemicals like acetone or alcohol are often used to remove the mask.

After this process is complete, the PCB is ready! The surface of the PCB will have thin copper lines on it called traces. The traces will be in the exact pattern of the mask that had been applied. Electronic components, like integrated circuits, can be attached to the PCB, and the traces will act like tiny wires that carry electricity between the components. The PCB, along with its components, can then be installed into an electronic device.

PRINTED CIRCUIT BOARD
© Trilobite | Dreamstime.com

You might not have thought that there is a connection between acids and computers, but acids are actually very useful for making the circuit boards that are common in today's computers. As computer technology continues to shrink, the ability to precisely etch circuits will become even more important.

4.5 Discussion questions

1. List as many items as you can think of that have PCBs (printed circuit boards) inside of them.

_____
_____
_____
_____
_____
_____
_____
_____
_____
_____
_____
_____

Chemistry connects to ......

2. Imagine what would happen if we did not have the ability to chemically etch computer boards. How would your life be different?

_____
_____
_____
_____
_____
_____
_____
_____
_____

3. What types of basic science information are needed to understand how etching works?

_____
_____
_____
_____
_____
_____
_____
_____
_____

5 Stomachs, Acids, and Protons

Technology

5.1 Acids inside you

5.2 Antacids

5.3 Other ways to control stomach acid

5.4 Discussion questions

5.1 Acids inside you

A chemist once claimed that he carried around a small amount of a very strong acid everywhere he went. He actually carried it inside his body! Does that sound shocking? As a matter of fact, you carry around the same acid! Your stomach produces hydrochloric acid (HCl). HCl helps your body digest the protein you eat.

One of the interesting things about your stomach is that it doesn't digest itself. There are glands in your stomach that produce mucus. The mucus in your stomach coats the lining. This mucus lining keeps the acid from damaging the inside surface of the stomach.

Sometimes a person's stomach produces too much acid. This can lead to a burning feeling called **acid indigestion**. Acid indigestion has many causes. These are some of the common causes of acid indigestion:

- eating too much rich/spicy food
- drinking too many carbonated beverages
- consuming a lot of caffeine
- stress

5.2 Antacids

The good news is that there are medications that can help treat acid indigestion. **Antacids** contain bases. They react with the extra stomach acid to neutralize it. Many antacids come in the form of tablets that can be chewed and then swallowed.

© Cammeraydave | Dreamstime.com

Remember that what makes acids "acidic" is the fact that they produce hydrogen (H^+) ions when they dissolve in water. Also remember that what makes bases "basic" is the fact that they produce hydroxide (OH^-) ions when dissolved in water. The HCl your stomach cells produce splits into hydrogen (H^+) ions and chlorine (Cl^-) ions. The bases in antacids give off OH^- ions that react with the H^+ ions to produce water (H_2O).

Many antacids contain calcium. Calcium is a mineral that is needed for healthy bones. Some antacid manufacturers even advertise that their products are good sources of calcium. Calcium ions combine with the chlorine ions that are "leftover" when HCl splits into ions. Your body can absorb this compound and use the calcium to strengthen your bones.

5.3 Other ways to control stomach acid

Antacids help control stomach acid when there is a little extra acid. Sometimes, however, the acid ends up in places where it isn't supposed to be. This can lead to serious damage to body tissues!

Sometimes, the stomach doesn't produce enough mucus to protect the lining of the stomach. If this happens, the stomach acid can actually start to digest the stomach itself! This leads to sores called **ulcers**.

Another common problem that occurs when stomach acid ends up in a place where it isn't supposed to be is called **acid reflux disease**. There is a tube that connects your mouth to your stomach; it is called an esophagus. At the end of your esophagus, there is a muscle that opens and closes your stomach. Sometimes this muscle doesn't work properly, and this leads to acid reflux. Acid reflux is when acid leaks up out of the stomach and into the esophagus. Your esophagus doesn't have as much mucus (as your stomach) to protect itself, so the acid starts to digest it.

Ulcers and acid reflux disease are serious medical conditions. Antacids can help with some of the symptoms, but they cannot cure these diseases. Fortunately, medical researchers have developed medications that can be used to treat ulcers and acid reflux. These medications work by controlling the amount of acid your stomach actually produces.

Remember that acids produce hydrogen (H⁺) ions. A hydrogen ion is basically just a proton. Hydrogen atoms have only one proton and one electron. If the hydrogen atom has a positive charge, this means that it has lost an electron. The result is a lone proton all on its own.

Doctors and medical researchers have developed a type of medication called a **proton pump inhibitor** (PPI). The stomach cells that produce HCl contain structures called "proton pumps." The proton pumps are part of the process of producing the acid. An **inhibitor** is a chemical that stops another chemical reaction from happening. So a proton pump inhibitor actually interferes with the way the stomach produces HCl. This means that less acid is produced. This, in turn, means that the acid that causes the ulcer or acid reflux is controlled, and this allows for healing to take place.

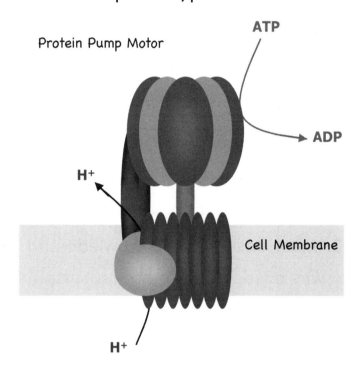

There are some possible problems associated with using PPIs. Some common side effects include stomach pain, diarrhea, and gas. But the damage to the stomach and esophagus that the PPIs can prevent is probably worth some minor discomfort! While it can cause problems if there is too much of it, the acid you carry with you is necessary for healthy digestion.

5.4 Discussion questions

1. What basic science knowledge (in chemistry, biology, and/or physics) was needed before antacids could be invented?

_____
_____
_____
_____
_____
_____
_____

2. What basic science knowledge (in chemistry, biology, and/or physics) was needed before proton pump inhibitors could be invented?

_____
_____
_____
_____
_____
_____
_____
_____
_____

3. Before chemistry, physics, and biology were used to invent new technologies in medicine, people discovered that many plants could be used to treat medical problems. What traditional remedies may have been used to treat indigestion, and why do you think they worked?

4. Discuss how traditional medicine has contributed to our understanding of science.

5. Discuss how science has contributed to our understanding of traditional medicines.

_____
_____
_____
_____
_____
_____
_____
_____
_____
_____

6 Ferrofluids Technology

6.1 Solutions vs. suspensions

6.2 Colloids—a special type of suspension

6.3 What is a ferrofluid?

6.4 Ferrofluid applications

6.5 Discussion questions

6.1 Solutions vs. suspensions

You've learned that homogeneous mixtures are made when one substance is dissolved in another. Dissolving results in a mixture called a **solution**. Think about dissolving a spoonful of sugar in a glass of water. If you pour the sugar into the water and stir, the sugar spreads out evenly in the water. This would be a **homogeneous mixture** because there is the same amount of sugar everywhere in the glass.

On the other hand, in **heterogeneous mixtures**, the particles are not spread out evenly. Think about a muddy stream. The flowing water keeps stirring up the mud and silt from the bottom of the stream. The current keeps the mud and silt mixed into the water. But what will happen if you draw a jar of muddy water out of the stream? At first, the water will have mud and silt floating in it.

Picture what will happen if you leave the jar set for a while. First, the biggest particles of sand will start to settle out. Then the smaller particles will settle out. Finally, the tiniest particles of dust will settle out, and you will be left with fairly clear water. There will be a layer of "sludge" on the bottom of the jar. Of course the sludge can easily be stirred up again, but the particles will eventually settle out again.

This muddy water mixture is a type of heterogeneous mixture that is called a **suspension**. The particles of sand and mud are suspended in the water, but they settle out over time. This settling that takes place in suspensions results in layers of different substances.

What determines whether a mixture will be a solution or a suspension? The size of the particles in the mixture is one factor. Generally, smaller particles (like sugar molecules) will spread out evenly and will create a solution. Larger particles (like sand or mud) are usually not able to spread out evenly; the result is a suspension.

Another factor that determines the organization of a mixture is the similarity of the substances that make up the mixture. Remember that **like dissolves like**. Sugar and water are relatively similar, so sugar will dissolve in water. Oil and water are not very similar, so they will separate into layers.

6.2 Colloids—a special type of suspension

It is usually easy to tell whether a mixture is a solution or a suspension. However, sometimes it isn't so simple. Some suspensions actually behave more like solutions! These special suspensions are called **colloids** (käl'-oidz).

A colloid is a suspension. However, it is made up of small particles, and it looks very much like a solution. A colloid is like an in-between mixture that is part homogeneous and part heterogeneous. The particles are very small, and they are spread out evenly; thus the colloid is like a solution. But the particles making up the mixture are not dissolved; the substances are not "alike." Colloids are unique suspensions because the substances do not settle out!

Whether or not you've heard of colloids before, you are likely familiar with some common examples. For instance, whipped cream is a colloid. Beating cream mixes air into it. The air doesn't dissolve in the cream, but it does spread out evenly throughout the cream. The mixed-in air is what makes whipped cream fluffy.

Another common example of a colloid is fog. Fog is a mixture of air and very tiny droplets of water. The water doesn't settle out of the air, but the droplets aren't dissolved in the air either.

Mayonnaise is another common colloid. Mayonnaise is a mixture that is made up of oil and vinegar. Of course, oil and vinegar won't stay mixed; vinegar is mostly made of water, and oil and water won't stay combined. However, if you add another chemical to the mixture, the oil and vinegar will stay mixed. Where can this incredible chemical be found? Egg yolks! Egg yolks contain a chemical that helps to keep the normally unmixable oil and vinegar nicely combined. This is what it takes for some colloids to stay together: a chemical added to the mixture to keep things combined.

6.3 What is a ferrofluid?

Can you picture trying to pick up a paperclip with a magnet? If you move the magnet close to the paperclip, the magnetic field surrounding the magnet affects the paper clip, and causes it to move. Now try to imagine a liquid that can be affected by a magnet. If you can picture it, you have a fairly good idea of what ferrofluids are like.

A ferrofluid is a type of suspension that contains a material that can be magnetized. But there is a problem. The magnetizable material that is used in a ferrofluid will settle out of the liquid. So there is another important ingredient that must be added to a ferrofluid. Remember mayonnaise? Egg yolks help to keep the other ingredients combined. A chemical called a **surfactant** is added to a ferrofluid to help keep the suspension mixed. The surfactant acts like the egg yolks do for the oil and vinegar. The surfactant keeps the small magnetizable particles from settling out of the liquid. The surfactant makes the ferrofluid suspension a colloid.

Ferrofluids are not magnets themselves, but magnets can affect them. For example, just like you can magnetize a nail with a magnet, ferrofluids can be magnetized by magnets. This makes them very useful materials!

6.4 Ferrofluid applications

Ferrofluids are a relatively new technology, but there are many ways they can be used. The first ferrofluids were invented by NASA for use in the early space program. The valves that controlled how rocket fuel was used contained ferrofluids. Magnets were used to magnetize the ferrofluids in the valves. The valves were then controlled (opened and closed) magnetically. Since their use in those early rockets, ferrofluids have found their way into many other common items.

Computer hard drives often contain ferrofluids that help to seal the drives in order to keep dust and other materials out. Sensors and switches in some electronic devices contain ferrofluids. By using magnets, these parts can be precisely controlled. Speakers sometimes contain ferrofluids. Magnets can affect the ferrofluids in the speakers to help control the shaking of the electronics inside. Some new kinds of shock absorbers in cars contain ferrofluids. If a magnet is used with these shock absorbers, computers built into the car can control the stability of the vehicle.

Researchers are also experimenting with some other less common and more amazing applications of ferrofluids. The U.S. Air Force is experimenting with using ferrofluids in the paints used on fighter jets. The ferrofluids help make the planes harder to see on radar. Some researchers are using ferrofluids to find more precise ways of producing lenses. Lenses for telescopes and microscopes must be polished carefully, and ferrofluids can be very accurately controlled to do this. Some medical researchers are even experimenting with using ferrofluids to help treat diseases like cancer. A ferrofluid can be injected into a cancerous tumor. When a strong magnetic field is applied, the ferrofluid moves around. This movement produces heat, which can kill the cancer cells!

6.5 Discussion questions

1. What basic science knowledge (in chemistry, biology, and/or physics) was needed before ferrofluids could be invented?

_____
_____
_____
_____
_____
_____
_____

2. Ferrofluids are being used in aeroscience and medicine – two completely different fields. Discuss how different applications of new technologies can contribute to more than one area of science.

_____
_____
_____
_____
_____
_____
_____

3. If you had a ferrofluid, what new application would you invent?

7 Gas Chromatography and Mass Spectrometry Technology

7.1 Complex mixtures

7.2 Gas chromatography and mass spectrometry

7.3 How are gas chromatography and mass spectrometry useful?

7.4 Discussion questions

7.1 Complex mixtures

Some mixtures are easier to separate than others. Your mom may complain that your room is a complex mixture, but you can easily hand sort the mess! But imagine a container of salt water. If you want to separate

the salt from the water, you cannot do it with your fingers. You will have to use some other technique. You can heat the mixture. If the water gets hot enough, it will boil. As it changes from a liquid to a gas, the steam (water in gas form) will spread out into the air, and the salt will be left behind. This technique is called **evaporation**.

But simple evaporation or hand sorting won't work for all mixtures. Generally speaking, more complex mixtures require more complex separation processes. Imagine a mixture of salt, sand, and iron filings. How could you separate such a mixture?

You could begin by using a magnet to remove the iron filings. Then you could mix the remaining salt and sand with water. This would dissolve the salt, but leave the sand. You might then filter this mixture. The salt water would flow through the filter, but the sand would be removed. Finally, you could boil the salt water to remove the water. The three parts of the original mixture would then be separated.

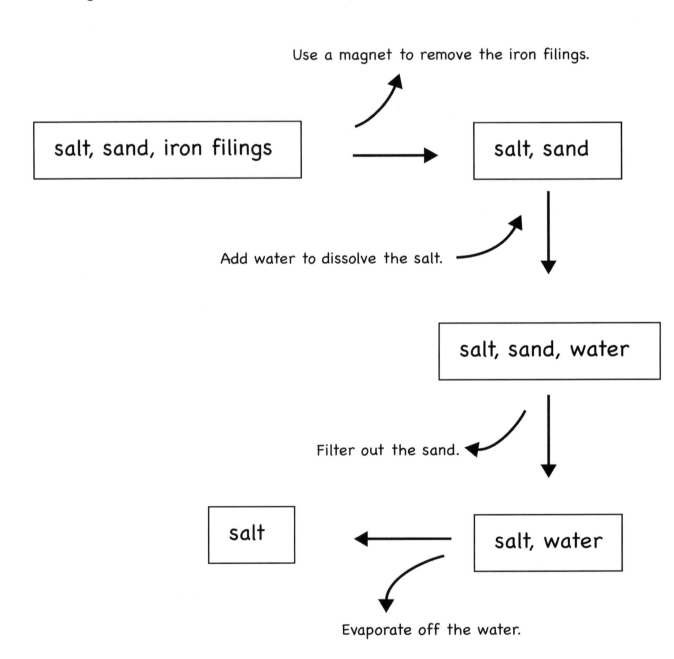

Of course, in this example, you were told what three things had been combined to make the mixture. This gave you some clues as to how you could separate the parts. Is it possible to separate a mixture if you don't even know what makes it up? How could you identify the parts of an "unknown" substance?

7.2 Gas chromatography and mass spectrometry

Chromatography is a broad term that is used to describe processes of separating mixtures. **Gas chromatography** is a form of chromatography that can be used to separate an unknown mixture into its separate parts.

The gas chromatography process begins when a small amount of the mixture is injected into a special kind of oven called a gas chromatograph. The oven heats the mixture to convert it into a gas. Many gas chromatography ovens can heat up to about 320° Celsius—about 600° Fahrenheit!

Inside the oven, helium gas is used to carry the now gaseous mixture through a tube. Helium gas is used to carry the mixture, because helium doesn't react chemically with other substances. The inside of the tube is coated with a special non-reactive coating so that it doesn't react with the gaseous mixture as it is carried through the tube.

The different parts of the gaseous mixture separate, and the parts are carried by the helium in the tube at different speeds. The speed at which the separated parts move depends on what they are. Smaller molecules will move faster than large ones.

Once the mixture is separated, another device can tell you what the parts actually are. This device is called a **mass spectrometer**. A beam of electrons blasts the separated parts of the mixture as they pass into the mass spectrometer. This causes them to become charged. The charged particles then pass through an electromagnetic field.

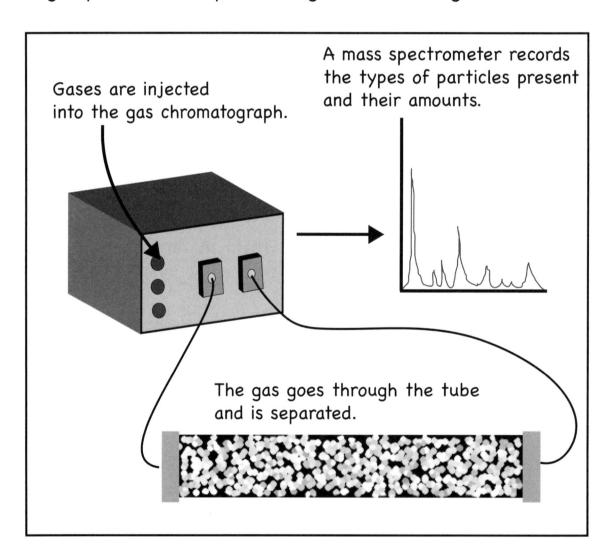

Gases are injected into the gas chromatograph.

A mass spectrometer records the types of particles present and their amounts.

The gas goes through the tube and is separated.

The electromagnetic field directs the particles through a filter, where the mass of the particles is measured. Remember that different particles have different masses. As particles pass through the filter, a detector keeps track of what types of particles pass through, as well as how many of them there are.

The information about the types and number of particles is sent to a computer. The computer creates a graph that shows the result. This graph is called a **mass spectrum**. The mass spectrum shows the composition of the original mixture. The mass spectrum graph looks like a series of peaks and valleys. Each peak represents one component of the mixture. The taller the peak, the more of that component there is in the mixture.

7.3 How are gas chromatography and mass spectrometry useful?

Being able to separate a mixture and identify its components has many useful applications. Researchers and scientists in fields as diverse as space exploration, archaeology, and forensic science use gas chromatography and mass spectrometry (GC-MS).

Since the 1970s, astronomers that have sent space probes to other planets have included GC-MS devices. The inclusion of these devices allows researchers to find out more about what the planets and their moons are like. The space probes can collect samples of the atmospheres and even samples of the surfaces of other planets and moons. The mass spectrums that are produced reveal the elements that are present on other planets and moons and in their atmospheres.

Archaeologists unearth historical artifacts that help us to better understand the past. They use GC-MS to determine how old the artifacts they find actually are. The process archaeologists employ to date the artifacts is called **radioactive isotope dating**. How does radioactive isotope dating work? Well, before answering that question, let's review the concept of isotopes. As you recall, each element has a specific number of protons in its nucleus. However, the number of neutrons present in an atom's nucleus can vary, and this variation creates different forms of an element. These different forms are called **isotopes**. Now, let's return to our question: How does radioactive isotope dating work? Well, the element carbon always has six protons. The number of neutrons, however, can vary. Most carbon atoms have six neutrons in their nuclei, but some have eight. The carbon atoms with six neutrons are called carbon-12, and the carbon atoms with eight neutrons are called carbon-14. Over time, carbon-14 will break down into carbon-12. Scientists know about how long it takes for this to happen. Archaeologists use a GC-MS to measure how much carbon-14 is left in an artifact. This tells them about how old the artifact is.

The field of forensic science employs scientific techniques to study evidence found at a crime scene. When investigators collect evidence from a crime scene, they sometimes need to perform what is called trace analysis. Trace analysis uses GC-MS to find out exactly what is in a small sample of a particular substance. For instance, imagine that an investigator finds a small puddle of a mysterious red liquid at a crime scene. Using GC-MS, a forensic scientist can tell if this red liquid is a deadly poison or a dangerous explosive or simply a melted Popsicle!

7.4 Discussion questions

1. What basic science knowledge (in chemistry, biology, and/or physics) was needed before the gas chromatograph could be invented?

___

2. What basic science knowledge (in chemistry, biology, and/or physics) was needed before the mass spectrometer could be invented?

___

3. Imagine all that is needed to use gas chromatography and mass spectrometry on a far away planet. If you were in charge of that project, what technological inventions would you need? List them.

8 Fats Technology

8.1 Fats in your food

8.2 What are lipids?

8.3 Hydrogenated fats

8.4 Developing alternative fuels from grease

8.5 Discussion questions

8.1 Fats in your food

Do you know how much fat is in that burger and fries? Oh, I'll have low-fat dressing on my salad. I know frozen yogurt has less fat than ice cream, but it just doesn't taste as good! Have you heard people say things like these?

Many people are concerned about eating too much fat. Fats are important substances in foods, and they are necessary for good health, but too much fat can have a negative affect on the body. It is not only how much fat that a person consumes that is important, but also, the types of fat that are consumed.

8.2 What are lipids?

There are many substances that we call lipids. Lipids are **organic molecules**. Organic molecules are any molecules that contain the element carbon and that are necessary for life. Carbohydrates and lipids are types of organic compounds. Carbohydrates and lipids are used to store up large amounts of energy for living things. Fats, oils, and waxes are all examples of lipids.

Lipids are often complex molecules that are made up of hundreds, or even thousands, of atoms. On one end of a lipid molecule, carbon, hydrogen, and oxygen atoms are bonded together. One the other end of a lipid molecule, there are long chains of carbon atoms, with hydrogen atoms attached. These long chains make up much of the lipid molecule.

Recall that carbon atoms make covalent bonds with other atoms. Usually, a carbon atom combines with four other atoms, because it has four electrons available for making bonds. To make up a lipid chain, a carbon atom can make shared electron bonds with two other carbon atoms and with two hydrogen atoms. Fats like these, in which the carbon atoms make four single bonds, are called **saturated fats.** The carbon chain looks something like this:

$$CH_2-CH_2-CH_2-CH_2-CH_2-CH_2-CH_2-CH_2-CH_2-CH_2-CH_2-CH_2-CH_2-CH_2$$

Sometimes though, the carbon chains take on a slightly different form. Sometimes, a carbon atom makes a single bond with one carbon atom and a double bond with another carbon atom. This leaves only one electron available to bond to a hydrogen atom. An example of this sort of carbon chain looks like this:

$$CH=CH-CH=CH-CH=CH-CH=CH-CH=CH-CH=CH-CH=CH$$

Notice that in this carbon chain, each carbon atom makes exactly four bonds. The two carbon atoms making the double bond can each bond with only one hydrogen atom. Fats that contain this sort of double bond are called **unsaturated fats.**

Unsaturated fats usually have a lower melting temperature than saturated fats. Compare vegetable oil and butter. Vegetable oil is a liquid at room temperature. This is because vegetable oil is made up of mainly unsaturated fats. Butter, on the other hand, is made of mostly saturated fats, so it tends to stay solid at room temperature.

8.3 Hydrogenated fats

Food scientists have found ways to make unsaturated fats (the ones that melt at low temperatures) behave more like saturated fats (the more "solid" ones). Margarine, for instance, is actually made of mostly unsaturated fats. It is really just vegetable oil that has been treated with a chemical to make it behave like a saturated fat. This is why you can spread margarine on your toast so easily.

The key to this process is adding hydrogen gas to the unsaturated fats. The process is called **hydrogenation**. During hydrogenation, unsaturated fats are heated up, and hydrogen is added. Then special metal brushes stir the mixture of fats and hydrogen, and some of the bonds change. When this happens, the unsaturated fats act more like saturated fats. Fats treated in this manner are sometimes called partially hydrogenated oils. Hydrogenated fats are very common in many processed foods.

The process of hydrogenation raises the melting temperature of the unsaturated fats and gives them a longer shelf life. For example, the grease used to fry french fries in fast-food restaurants is often a partially hydrogenated vegetable oil. This grease is packaged in cartons, and it has a whitish, semi-solid form. As the solid grease heats up in the fryer, it melts into golden-brown liquid oil. Using a hydrogenated oil allows the restaurants to more easily transport and store the oil that they will need in the future.

Unfortunately, the use of hydrogenated fats has drawbacks. The process of hydrogenation causes the molecules of fat to change shape into forms that are easily stored up in the human body. Also, using hydrogenated fats can be expensive, because of the processing that is involved.

8.4 Developing alternative fuels from grease

Imagine how much hydrogenated oil is used in all of the fast food restaurants in this country every day. What happens to it? Most of this frying grease is waste, and it ends up getting thrown away, because it can't be reused.

Some researchers have come up with a pretty amazing idea for what to do with this used frying grease. Chemists have found that this waste vegetable oil (WVO) is similar to diesel fuel, chemically speaking. Once it has been filtered and purified, the WVO will burn quite well, and it can be used as a replacement for diesel fuel!

There is a slight problem with this. Think about how "thick" vegetable oil is. Scientists use the term "viscosity" to describe the thickness of a liquid. WVO is much more viscous than normal diesel fuel. Remember that hydrogenated fats act more like saturated fats, and they have a higher melting point!

Because WVO is "thicker" than diesel fuel, it actually can't be used immediately after filtering to power a diesel engine. It is just too viscous! But, if the WVO is heated, it becomes less viscous, and it can be burned just like diesel fuel. Engines that can use WVO for fuel are usually specially designed with two fuel tanks. One tank contains regular diesel fuel, and this fuel is used to start the engine. As the engine warms up, the heat thins out the WVO in the second fuel tank. Once the engine is warmed up, the WVO from the second tank is used instead.

Turning waste vegetable oil into a fuel is a great way to help take care of the earth. Restaurants are happy to get rid of their WVO, and using WVO as a fuel means that less of it ends up being thrown away, because it has value! Further, burning WVO produces less waste carbon dioxide gas than burning diesel. And by using WVO as a fuel, people can reduce the amount of petroleum-based fuel they need.

8.5 Discussion questions

1. What basic science knowledge (in chemistry, biology, and/or physics) was needed before margarine could be invented?

78   Chemistry connects to ......

2. What basic science knowledge (in chemistry, biology, and/or physics) was needed before waste grease could be used as fuel for trucks?

3. Imagine that you are in charge of getting rid of waste restaurant grease, but you can't use it as diesel fuel. What would you do?

9 Synthetic Fabrics Technology

9.1 Synthetic fibers

9.2 Nomex

9.3 Kevlar

9.4 Discussion questions

9.1 Synthetic fibers

What are your clothes made out of? Check the labels sometime. Many pieces of clothing are made of cotton, which is a natural fiber. Natural fibers are materials that come from living things. Linen and wool are other examples of natural fibers; linen is made from a plant called flax, and wool comes from sheep.

If you look carefully through your closet or drawers, however, you are likely to find some clothes that are not made entirely of natural fibers. Some clothes are made of synthetic fibers. Synthetic means that people create them. Synthetic fibers are not found in nature. Instead, they are made by researchers in laboratories.

The first synthetic fiber ever created was made in 1939. It was created by a researcher who was working for the DuPont Corporation, a large chemical company. The substance was named **nylon**.

Nylon is a polymer. It is made up of long repeating chains of shorter molecules. Nylon is made by combining two different molecules. To make nylon, you pour one chemical on top of another. This creates a layer on top of another layer. Nylon is formed right at the border between the layers. The nylon can be drawn out from the liquid as a thread. The nylon thread must be dried before it can be used.

When nylon was first invented, scientists weren't exactly sure what to do with it. In the years since 1939, researchers have found thousands of uses for this amazing polymer! Nylon has been used for toothbrush bristles, ropes, car parts, fishing line, parachutes, strings for musical instruments, hoses, dental floss, tents, sleeping bags, seat belts, and (of course) all sorts of clothes and shoes. The most famous use of nylon is probably women's pantyhose. They are often called nylons!

Other synthetic fibers have been invented since the time that nylon was created in 1939. These include acrylic, Dacron, polyester, spandex, Nomex, and Kevlar. All of these are different polymer compounds. The last two, in particular, have some interesting properties and uses.

9.2 Nomex

Imagine that you could put on a suit and then run through fire without getting burned. Sounds like something from the movies, right? Actually it is! Hollywood stuntmen sometimes wear special suits under their costumes to prevent accidental burns when they perform. These suits are made of a substance called Nomex.

Nomex is a polymer that can be made into useful materials. It was invented by the DuPont Corporation in the 1960s. The most incredible property of Nomex is that it is extremely resistant to heat. This makes it useful for all sorts of applications.

Nomex can be made into cloth. This cloth is both lightweight and fire resistant. Nomex does not burn well at all. If it does catch fire, it will stop burning as soon as the heat source is removed. Nomex also resists heat very well. Therefore, a person wearing Nomex is afforded some protection from high heat sources. So, while it is not completely fireproof, a Nomex suit will help protect the person who is wearing it.

© Rhonda Odonnell | Dreamstime.com

Firefighters often wear Nomex suits to help keep them safe when they are rescuing people from burning buildings. Racecar drivers wear Nomex suits under their racing jumpsuits. This helps to protect them from burns in case they crash. Military pilots wear Nomex flight-suits for the same reason.

Nomex can also be rolled into sheets. Sheets of Nomex can be formed into all sorts of shapes. This makes it useful for all sorts of products for which controlling heat is important.

Some car parts can be made from Nomex, and this makes cars that contain these parts safer. Parts made from Nomex are less likely to melt or burn than parts made from other polymers.

Electrical wires can be insulated with Nomex. Insulation is the plastic (polymer) coating around the outside of the wire. When large amounts of electrical charge are passing through a wire, the wire can get very hot! Nomex insulation is less likely to melt than other polymers. Because Nomex is also lightweight and strong, Nomex is used for making airplane engine parts and tail fins, and it is used for making helicopter blades.

9.3 Kevlar

Imagine being a soldier about to head into battle. Wouldn't it be nice if you could wear a suit that is strong enough to stop a bullet? Such a suit could save your life! Thankfully, there is such a suit; it is made of a polymer called Kevlar.

Kevlar was also invented by researchers at DuPont. (DuPont scientists have made some pretty incredible chemical discoveries

© Robert Mizerek | Dreamstime.com

over the years!) It is incredibly strong. For the same weight, Kevlar is five times stronger than steel! A soldier wearing a suit of Kevlar body-armor can be saved from a deadly bullet, without being totally weighed down. Because it is so incredibly strong and lightweight, Kevlar is an incredibly useful polymer. Kevlar is being used in many different ways.

- Kevlar is used to make bulletproof vests for police officers and soldiers.
- Kevlar can be used to make the cables that support bridges. Because Kevlar is much lighter than steel, but equally strong, a bridge with Kevlar cables can be made lighter, without compromising the strength of the bridge. Also, Kevlar does not rust or corrode like many metals.
- Kevlar is used to make protective equipment for industrial workers. Factory workers who work with glass or sheet metal might suffer a serious cut if they wear gloves that are made out of regular cloth. Kevlar gloves, however, are very difficult to cut or tear. Kevlar gloves and clothing can help keep the workers safe.
- Parts for cars and airplanes can be made lighter and stronger by using Kevlar instead of other materials. Tires, brake pads, belts, hoses, and even parts of the vehicle body can be made from Kevlar.
- Many types of sports equipment are now made with Kevlar. Snowboards, tennis rackets, canoes, hiking boots, hockey sticks, baseball bats, bicycles, and sailboats are all made lighter and stronger using Kevlar.

Polymers have unique properties that make them useful as synthetic fabrics. Fabrics like Nomex and Kevlar just don't grow on trees! These amazing synthetic fabrics make our lives safer and more comfortable.

9.4 Discussion questions

1. What basic science knowledge (in chemistry, biology, and/or physics) was needed before nylon, Nomex, and Kevlar could be made?

_____
_____
_____
_____
_____
_____
_____
_____
_____
_____
_____
_____
_____
_____

2. Imagine that you have invented a new polymer. List the properties of your polymer below. (Here are some things to consider: Can it be cut? Is it nonflammable? Can it serve as a cloak of invisibility? etc.)

_____   _____
_____   _____
_____   _____
_____   _____
_____   _____
_____   _____

3. What would you make out of your new polymer? How would it be used?

_____
_____
_____
_____
_____
_____
_____
_____
_____

10 Polymerase Chain Reaction Technology

10.1 DNA structure

10.2 Copying DNA

10.3 DNA testing and PCR

10.4 Discussion questions

10.1 DNA Structure

You've learned that proteins and DNA are polymers that are present inside of living cells. Proteins do all sorts of things for your cells. DNA, on the other hand, does only one thing. It is designed to carry information. The information held in your DNA tells your cells how to make all of the different kinds of protein that your body needs.

Remember the shape of DNA? It looks sort of like a twisted ladder. The "sides" of the ladder are chains of deoxyribose (sugar) groups that give DNA its shape and structure. The "rungs" of the ladder are made up of pairs of genetic bases. The names of the bases are abbreviated A, C, G, and T. Remember that A always pairs up with T, and C always pairs up with G. These bases are bonded strongly to the sugar groups and weakly to each other. Your DNA bases come in a particular pattern that is called your genome.

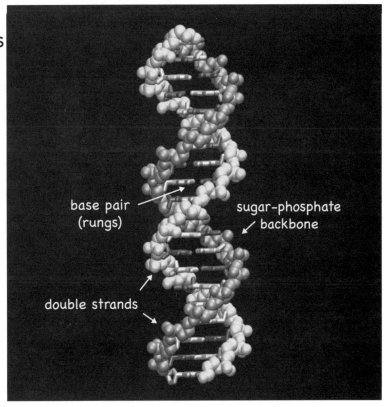

Your genome is made up of sections of DNA called genes. Each gene tells your cells how to make a certain type of protein. One gene might tell your pancreas cells to produce an enzyme to help break down food. Another gene might tell your muscle cells to make proteins that give your muscles structure. Still another gene might tell your eye cells how to make proteins that give your eyes their color. Every living thing has DNA that carries information for how to make the proteins that each living thing needs.

You inherited your genes from your mother and your father. This means that you have characteristics that you inherited from your parents. For example, if you have brown eyes, it means you inherited a gene that told your eye cells to produce a protein that causes your eyes to be brown.

Why are genes important? The particular combination of genes in your DNA is what makes you unique! The order of your DNA bases is different from the order of your best friend's DNA bases. Dogs and cats and oak trees and bacteria and people all have different orders of DNA bases.

10.2 Copying DNA

The shape of the DNA molecule is very important! Its unique shape allows DNA to easily copy itself. Why is this important? Remember that DNA is inside of living cells. When cells reproduce, each new cell needs a complete copy of the DNA.

When cells reproduce, the DNA "ladder" splits in two. The weak bonds between the bases are broken, and the DNA molecule "unzips" down the middle. A special protein called DNA polymerase "reads" the bases of each half-strand of DNA and adds the bases and sugars to complete each strand. (Remember, A always matches up with T, and C always matches up with G!) The result is two complete, identical DNA molecules.

10.3 DNA Testing and PCR

You've probably heard of "DNA testing." Geneticists (scientists who study genes) use DNA tests to find where particular genes are located in a living thing's DNA. Crime lab technicians use DNA tests on evidence found at crime scenes. Sometimes, the results of the DNA tests reveal the identity of the person who committed the crime. Doctors can use DNA tests to determine whether a patient might get a particular genetic disease.

When scientists want to do a DNA test, they need a fairly large amount of DNA to test. The problem is that usually they start with a very, very small sample of DNA. However, in 1983 a scientist named Kary Mullis developed a way of making many copies of DNA. The method is called the polymerase chain reaction (PCR). In 1993, Mullis won the Nobel Prize in Chemistry for his discovery.

Imagine that a researcher wants to copy a particular gene to test it. When using PCR, the researcher begins with a strand of DNA that contains the gene. This section of DNA is called the target sequence.

The researcher places the DNA in a sterile test tube, along with a few chemicals that are needed for PCR to take place:
- Primers – These are small snippets of DNA that match the beginning of the DNA target sequence.
- A polymerase – The polymerase "reads" the target sequence and fills in the matching bases.
- Additional bases – The polymerase matches these with the target sequence to complete the strand of DNA.

The first step of PCR is called **denaturing**. In this step, the tube is heated. The added heat causes the weak bonds between the DNA's bases to break. The two strands of the "twisted ladder" unwind and separate.

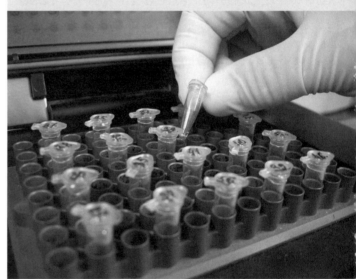
© Victorpr | Dreamstime.com

The next step is called **annealing**. In this step, the temperature of the mixture is reduced. This allows the primers to attach to the target sequence. The polymerase attaches to the DNA strand at the primer.

The third step is called **extension**. Now the polymerase moves along the strand of DNA and adds the matching bases to complete the strand. This results in two complete strands of DNA that contain the target sequence.

PCR repeats these three steps over and over again. The DNA is denatured, the primers are annealed, and the polymerase extends the primers by adding bases to complete the target sequence. After repeating these steps 30 times, there are more than a million copies of the target sequence, which is plenty of DNA to test!

10.4 Discussion questions

1. What basic science knowledge (in chemistry, biology, and/or physics) was needed before PCR could be invented?

2. PCR is often used in criminal investigations. List some advantages and disadvantages PCR may have for criminal investigations.

___

3. The cell is full of little motors like the polymerase motor that makes PCR possible. One such machine is called a kinase; it cuts strands of DNA. Imagine that you could modify the kinase to cut anything. What technology might you create with such tiny scissors?

___